The Secrets
of Business

for young entrepreneurs

by Alex Falcon-Huerta

The Secrets of Business for Young Entrepreneurs

Copyright © Alex Falcon-Huerta, 2020

First published 2020 by Falcon Huerta Press

ISBN: 978-1-5272-7440-2

Edited by Richard Sergeant
Design and Typeset by Loulita Gill Design

A CIP catalogue record for this book is available from the British Library.

Hey, it's me, Alex,

I love being in business, and I love helping people get their own ideas off the ground and then supporting them as they grow.

I've written this book so I can share some of my experiences with those of you who are looking to set up a business, or have already started and are in the early stages. It won't give you any short cuts, but it will show you that your journey is real and that there are lessons to be learned that might just help get you through it more confidently.

It's not an easy ride, and it's not for everyone - but there are literally millions of people who want to be their own boss, and and build something that allows them to do great work and be rewarded for it. But they all need help along the way.

This book is designed to pick up and put down, dip in and out and not worry about remembering every bit - it's another friend you can draw on when you need. It could, I hope, also trigger ideas and thoughts that you'll have confidence to turn into actions and make a real difference to hitting your goals.

Some things will make sense now, and some won't resonate for a while, but rest assured that it's always good to know others have been there before, and to feel that you're already ahead.

Good luck on your journey!

ALEX

Foreword

by Rod Drury, Founder, Xero,

By sharing the lessons she has learned along her journey, Alex wants you to succeed.

As a leader in our global community Alex has shown she understands the enthusiasm, drive and determination that young entrepreneurs have - and knows that you need a broader range of skills and a bigger perspective on things in order to survive and thrive.

Having built several international businesses over the years, I'm a believer in learning from the experiences of others, being able to listen, and making the right decisions early on.

Making time to read this book and absorb the many gems Alex shares from her journey might be one of the most valuable things you can do to give you the confidence to grow, and improve things for your customers, your business and yourself.

Contents

1

Be An Entrepreneur

Once you start a
business you'll
wonder why the hell
you didn't do it
before.

Learning as a 'young' entrepreneur never stops

Once you've made the great escape, and become an entrepreneur you will wonder why you didn't do it before.

Anyone who isn't wants to be one, and anyone who is thrives on it.

It's an opportunity to use your creativity, your drive, your ambition and be who you want to be. You are never too young or even too old to start up your own venture.

As 'young' entrepreneurs you might not be as fearless as the older generation - but you've got the right to do things your own way!

Just NEVER stop learning.

You're on a journey where there is no final destination - keep an open mind, watch, learn, and grow into your role as a leader and business person.

Set your launch date

Once you've made the decision that you want to start your own business - be brave. Pick a date to launch and plan back from there to work out what you need to do.

There will be a lot to think about so actually making yourself accountable to a fixed date means you will take action.

Give yourself the satisfaction of working towards something, putting milestones in place to map your achievements.

Being an entrepreneur and new business owner is both exciting and scary. But having a clear plan, and a clear date helps to keep you on track and grounded.

Take the best bits

Setting up on your own can be scary, but it's also fresh oxygen.

You've been so wrapped in the bubble of politics and pleasing people, when you come out it's like you've been living in another world.

You might want to throw it all away and start again but instead think about the processes, systems, discipline, culture and approach that you have been using and lean on the bits that have worked

As you scale your own business, you start to realise why some things you were made to do previously were there in the first place. Now, you'll need to start the cycle again with your team.

You'll also get there faster if you can work with an approach that is familiar, and that you are now the master of and can mold to exactly how you want.

Start with the right customers

It's far too easy to end up with the 'wrong' customers, even if you're absolutely clear on who you want to serve and why.

This can be a real drain on what little time and resource you have, and could be holding you back from making better and more important strides. Even worse if they aren't paying you the right rate for the work you are providing.

Have a strict criteria on who you want to work with, and do your utmost to stick to it.

The customers you end up with need to be quality ones who have a better chance of delivering real life time value - rather than sucking you dry.

Even as your business develops it's important to stay brave and keep to your criteria, letting go of unprofitable or wrong fit customers along the way frees you to add value to those you want to truly serve.

And never put up with people who disrespect you.

Look for the support you need

It can sometimes feel like a lonely place when responsibility for everything falls to you.

So, the people you surround yourself during these times can make all the difference.

Look to those you know and trust to give an impartial view or just be a friendly ear who can listen; or find entrepreneurial communities online where it's easy to share experiences and advice.

Generally people who have set up their own business have a genuine desire to help or mentor, give tips, and offer guidance.

There's no reason to be alone, you just need to step out, make those connections and ask.

2

No Excuses

You'll have to work
hard to make it all
work. Embrace it!

Don't follow the crowd

--- --- --- --- --- --- --- --- --- --- --- --- --- --- --- --- --- --- ---

Being different is a badge of honor, a brand statement, and a chance to offer something that others can't.

Take inspiration from the people you admire, the books you read, and conferences you go to but don't follow the crowd. Find your own way.

People are different, personalities are different, visions, goals, structures, systems. In other words no two businesses run exactly the same.

So, take the best from the best, and implement what you feel and think is right for you. You'll naturally develop your own style and ways of doing things.

Believe in yourself and what you want to achieve.

Carve your niche in the world, and an identity that your customers will want to be associated with.

Get stuff done

Getting stuff done is my key to everything in life.

It's easy to avoid dealing with things that we don't like doing or difficult situations, but we also forget about the consequences of not acting.

When your business is getting going it's really hard to stay on top of things, but that's no excuse. You've got to find a way to keep delivering for customers, to give you the time to do the things you want to do, and to keep you sane.

Not acting can mean not delivering on your service promise to customers, a damaged relationship and possibly a loss of income.

Keep organised, delegate and outsource as much as possible

Getting stuff done, doesn't mean you have to do it all yourself, it just means you find the best way to get it done without breaking yourself.

Follow your instincts

We all have those times when something doesn't feel quite right - and usually you're correct!

So use it.

Have a criteria or plan in mind when you have meetings, meet new people or make decisions, keep an open mind and go with your gut.

I sometimes go against my instincts - almost like I'm testing myself - and then later wish I hadn't!

So, get to know that feeling, and trust yourself to be right.

Slam the expectation gap

Challenges and issues are great opportunities.

If something has gone wrong - perhaps in delivering part of your service - embrace it.

It's likely that if it's happened once, it's going to happen again...and again. Learn from it, adapt where you can, and develop training for the team.

Making improvements to help one part of your business could also open up the chance to rethink how you do other things too.

If you can close a gap, SLAM it closed and turn that weakness into another strength.

Build your profile...quickly

Potential customers have to get to know who you are and how you can help them, while at the same time you can't wait forever to get new business in.

Building your profile quickly so you can attract customers as soon as possible becomes a priority.

Social media and lots of networking really helped get me there quicker - all of which are relatively low cost and in your control.

Business will come to you, but you've got to be a magnet for it - and that means getting out there and grabbing attention.

3

Book It, Do It

Discipline is really important if you're going to do the right thing for your customers, your business and yourself.

Time discipline

Planning keeps you on track.

Don't pay lip service to it, make it core to what you do every day.

Cramming everything in is a trap easily fallen into in the early days of your business. The reality is that even basic planning can go a very long way and helps you to prioritise.

Even when I did my exams I scheduled everything! I planned the week, the month, the term. I planned my work and my social time. I made sure I could see how I was spending my time and working towards my goals without driving myself into the ground.

In business it's been an essential discipline to keep going.

Book it in

Providing customers, staff, and family with a way of getting what they need from you, will help prevent you being dragged in lots of different directions at once.

Physically booking things into your diary and sticking to it makes you consistent and your day more predictable.

It allows others a way of booking time with you and for you to operate with few distractions.

It's your time, you have to look after it.

Delivering under pressure

THE most important thing is delivery to your customer.

They are the ones who pay the bills, meet the salaries and give the profit you need to stay in business.

You can't afford to drop the ball even when things get really busy, so have the tools and processes in place to cope.

Book the time needed into your diary.

Turn off notifications on your social apps

'Get stuff done' and action in full.

If you aren't going to deliver as promised then manage expectations as soon as possible. Let the customer know and let them know when they can expect it.

Simple little things like this greatly reduces pressure and stress on both sides.

Hot on delivery

Your reputation is always on the line, and beating customer expectations is about fast AND quality delivery.

As the owner you will work hard at both, but you'll have to constantly lead and demonstrate this to your team to help them become high performing too.

Your aim is to make this a part of the 'natural way' of working every day.

And it will happen. Especially as you will be able to draw a direct line between the amazing work that they do and customer satisfaction.

Happy customers are also repeat customers, and the most willing to refer others to you.

Book in time just for you

Life can be complex, challenging and hard work, so I HAVE to book in time to do my own thing.

And I literally book it in so it's there in black and white for all to see.

It's up to me how I use that time - an afternoon with friends or a long weekend away - but I know once it's in the diary it will happen.

Finding a balance is a recurring theme as your life can't all be about work.

Making the time to focus just on you and not the 101 things that you can end up carrying around in your head, will give you the breathing space to think clearer and help restore your strength.

4

Business Finances

Your business
is there to make
a profit so you
can do the things
you love. Being
in control of the
numbers is an
essential part of
getting there.

Learn the finance basics

- -

Many people go into business without knowing what the basics of finances are, but don't be one of them.

Gross margin, net margin, cost of investment, return on investment. They all sound abstract but you can pick up a book and learn super fast.

It's even better if you can book yourself on a basic finance course to learn about how to at least keep track of your income and outgoings in a systematised way.

The more you know, the more you will stay in control.

The most successful businesses are those that understand the finances, and can react to what the numbers are showing them.

Your head isn't the best accounting system

It's almost impossible to know where your finances are just by having it all in your head.

You'll know what should come in, what should go out and what costs you have personally to cover, but that's no way to run a business.

After you've got to grips with the basics of finance, get it out of your head and use some basic cloud accounting software.

Remember HMRC will expect you to be keeping an accurate record, and may ask you for this information in the future.

Keep a log, keep receipts, and keep it digital.

Budgeting and cash flow

Cash is THE most important thing to a business, especially in the early days.

Having a plan (budget), even if it's just a guide at first can give you a sense of direction, and becomes an essential part of planning as your business grows.

Plot out a month by month estimate of income and expenditure (ideally broken down by categories e.g salaries, software), and then regularly track what you spend on each. Do this daily at the beginning until you get an understanding of where you are, and even consider using cashflow add on software for your cloud accounting system to help.

Just writing these up or asking for expert help is essential to any business as it gives you the numbers you need to understand how well your business is doing and where changes or focus is needed.

See budgeting as an essential business as well as financial discipline.

Tax is a cost like any other

We all have to pay tax.

And yep, it's easy when you're on a salary as your employer just takes it before you get to see it hit your bank account.

But when it's your business tax becomes your problem.

So many people end up spending the money they should be putting to one side for their tax bill, and wonder why they end up in some kind of financial trouble at the end of the year.

My advice is to have another separate business account where you can safely save away what you think you need for tax so you don't have to worry about it when it's due.

Even a rough calculation is fine to start with, or better still, work with an accountant to agree what this figure should be. You should also let them produce your tax returns to ensure you don't pay more than you have to.

5

Technology

Choosing your tech isn't a one time decision, it's a never ending process.

Start right, think tech

A business that doesn't use the right tech will be hard to run and hard to scale.

Having a manual process also increases the chance of human error, so it pays to get your tech in place as soon as possible.

Break your business down into processes, and shortlist two providers for each by doing the research and checking out reviews.

Check functionality, user friendliness, scalability, and whether it connects to other tools you use. What do you think of their support? Is there a good community online that you can tap into?

Also make sure their charging model works for you. Price per user is OK to begin with but what about when you scale? Also watch out for fixed fee elements or added costs for features that you'll need.

If there's a lot you think you need, start with the basics - the essentials - and build from there.

Not all about the price

Controlling your costs is an essential discipline - and there's no need to be taken for a ride by tech providers.

However, price can't be the number one priority, even if you're just getting up and running.

There are products coming out all the time which are slick, user friendly and more aligned with today's way of working. So, it's not about price, it's about what is best for you and how you want to work.

In fact I would prioritise its ability to scale, easily add users, connections to other tech, and a clear development road map before price.

There's an advantage of course if there are a few products that offer similar functionality, and comparing prices in that competitive market can work in your favour.

Also it's worth remembering that it's never impossible to move software, even if you think you're totally reliant on something. I've moved key tech several times so that I can scale and serve a global market confidently.

Have your list ready and make sure it ticks all the boxes. Don't downgrade your business because a product doesn't match your needs..

Adapt to stay relevant

Tech always evolves and usually for the better: the interface may change, new features added, or the scope of what it does may widen. And that's what you want to see, right?

Well...it changes, but so do you.

I've changed major software apps several times over the years, just to match our needs and requirements within the business.

It's way too easy to get comfortable with what you've got.

Use all that choice in the market to your advantage.

Business continuity basics

Make sure your business can withstand serious interruption or a disaster. If the building goes up in smoke you still need to be able to serve your customers.

Work through the scenarios from a physical disaster to IT security breach to create comprehensive checklists of action to help prevent now, and what to do if it did still happen in the future.

Having your key systems and data in the cloud is an obvious step - but also make sure that you have confidence that your providers are robust and have their own plans in place.

Be cautious about very new players in the market, and do some careful checking around their growth, investors and ability to keep going in the long term - especially if you intend to use them for a critical function.

Account Managers

Having strong allies within your suppliers can pay surprising dividends.

A great relationship with your account manager helps to ensure that you get the support you need to use the product to its full potential. And when you get stuck, or if you need to do something quite quickly, they should be able to deal with it fast.

Nurturing these relationships can also lead to being used as a case study or showcase for their product - all great PR and marketing, and handy for boosting your profile.

I've been involved in videos which have a global audience which is insane! Over time it's also led to speaking gigs, appearances on expert panels, and writing articles all of which has helped me increase my reach.

Good account managers, especially in tech companies, move up the ladder very quickly and often become decision makers.

If you've managed to keep that close relationship it can often open more doors than you can first imagine.

6

Being The Boss

Stepping up to
become an employer
and having your
own team, comes
with all kinds of
challenges.

People make and complicate culture

Creating a culture that is *right* from the start is easy as most of it comes directly from you.

The challenges come when you have to combine it with the people you employ.

If these are in line then things are a lot easier, but they will still look to you to understand the goals and visions for the business.

Whatever your approach, agreeing between all of you that this is a way you want to work is essential.

Get it right and they'll come with you on your journey, no matter how crazy the idea.

Sometimes it may work, others it's going to fail, but showing them that they are involved and you're listening to their ideas reveals that it's possible to *try* - and that can be really inspiring.

Codify your approach as values, mantras, or just the rules of the game. The end result will be that the team knows exactly what is required, what part they play and how important they are to help the business achieve its targets.

No 9-5

We operate in a global environment, and that means that it's no longer a 9-5 job.

If your customers are everywhere you need to organise your team and make sure they understand that this may be an 'around the clock' business - meaning they may need to pitch in wherever and whenever they need to.

That's the reality of startup life.

Your job in return is to always ensure its fair, flexible and wellbeing isn't taken for granted.

Get rid fast

I can talk about this in some detail. But I won't...

Let's just say that if the person you hired isn't right, make a decision on it fast. It's better to focus on the right people than being drained by the wrong people.

Humans come with attitude, emotions and ideas

Treating people like robots and just expecting them to get on with the job will get you nowhere.

Knowing that you hired the right people means you have to also accept that they come with ideas, inspiration and thoughts on how things could be improved.

OK, it can be really testing (especially if everyone is really busy) but it shouldn't ever be a negative. Listen carefully and consider their ideas, in fact encourage more outside the box thinking.

It may be useful to book in time with them to go through things in more detail, and often that bit of distance can help you prepare and to think more clearly about what they are suggesting.

Ignoring people's needs and wants can be a recipe for disaster, so listening to those who speak up will help challenge you and the business to improve and grow.

Quality pays the bills

Your business needs structure, policies and procedures so everyone knows what's expected of them and to maintain high standards of delivery.

If things slipped I used to play it down and be very sympathetic, but you know sometimes it's just not good enough.

If someone in your team can't see this then act fast and make sure you follow a defined process of warnings.

Take a breath to make sure that internal changes aren't also needed, but don't let things slide. Make the changes, make improvements and always strengthen processes.

Your customers, reputation and quality is what pays the bills.

7

Working At Your Networking

Get out there and
find the right
people to help
you and your
business grow

Network for a reason

Networking is the best way to build connections that can make a big difference to your business.

But take a long hard look at the events you are thinking of attending: be selective and have a clear purpose as to why you're going.

You can waste a lot of time and cash trying to be everywhere, and you really don't need to.

Once you've decided - just go for it. Get there early, engage with others, ask questions, and find the key people to you and your purpose.

In business I'm always thinking about how I can get somewhere faster or do something better, and believe me it's not always by my method!

So I love finding out experts in their field who can help me. I would much rather use them than guess and waste even more time.

Working on your networking

- -

It's easy to get to know people at networking events.

But, it's hard to get lots of value from just listening to one pitch after another.

It's a lot easier if you're able to take a genuine interest, and have a chance to get to know them more personally.

Try to get people in one to one conversations so you can get to know their story and uncover what they are trying to achieve - your aim is to look for common ground and ways you can help each other.

They may just want an intro to someone, which is OK., as there could be a time when that's exactly what you'll need in return.

If you think there is something there to develop then swap contact details and agree on a time to catch up before you move on to the next person.

Social media

Not all of my posts are to do with business, but I do it with a personal brand and personality. This has a lot to do with attracting like minded people and remembering that people work with people they like.

You can really make this work for you if you also keep an eye on data which helps reveal what is working and where your best prospects are hanging out online.

Evolve your posts by considering how much time you spend on each platform, how you want to be perceived, and what will have the most impact on those you want to attract.

This will ensure the time you spend on social will be as much about marketing as it is about just getting you, as a key person, out there.

Find your heroes

In any business there will be people you look up to and have been influenced by.

What is it that they do that you like so much?

The people I would consider my influencers changed after I set up the business. I started to seek out those who had been there and done it all, because all of a sudden their advice was super valuable to me.

I would pay attention to their strategies and analyse their approach, implementing ideas directly into the business because I felt confident that they were workable models.

Learning from your heroes is a way of not having to work everything out for yourself, and provide tried and tested methods ready to take off the shelf.

Meet new circles of people

You can get so far from your existing network, but getting to know a whole new circle of people can give you an important advantage and keep things fresh.

Stepping out of your comfort zone by attending events builds confidence and makes the next time easier.

The main thing is to remember that you are there for a reason: to build connections, be noticed, and meet people who can help you on your journey or solve a specific issue.

If you get a chance then attending international events can be a huge advantage. Not only do you meet people from outside of your network but you also learn what others are doing to innovate in different countries.

It can be intimidating at first but put your ego to one side and your nerves in a box for a couple of hours and just do it.

8

Staying Relevant

Think your idea is great now? What will others think in two years time?

Think into the future

You can't become complacent in business, so thinking ahead needs to become second nature.

What you're doing now will only be relevant or effective for a short time, so you'll either have to change or have change forced on you by circumstances.

Think about what your future looks like - Where do you want to be?

What will your customers be looking for?
How is your market evolving?
What is technology doing to change things?
What will your staff need?

What is going to keep you relevant?

Regularly thinking through questions like these should become a natural part of your thinking and planning.

Do things others can't see

- -

If you can spot a gap, and the opportunity excites you, then go for it.

In a crowded market place competition is always tough - and no one owes you any favours.

Finding that bit of clear space could set you apart from the crowd and give you the edge needed to create a distinctive brand or offering.

If you can grab those opportunities it will be too late for your competitors to do anything but play catch up - by which time you need to have moved on!

No standing still

You may be at the very front of what you do right now, but this won't last forever.

The people who are important to your business now are unlikely to be the same in 10 or even 5 years time.

Your customer base will change, your staff will change and everyone will become younger as you get older!

Staying relevant to all these key people is something you have to work hard on if your business is going to keep on flourishing.

Keeping up to date with what's happening in your world, and theirs will help keep you ahead.

Spend time researching, speak to your employees, speak to your customers, and turn those conversations into ideas and innovations.

9

(Re)Train Your Brain

Develop positive
habits that
reduce stress and
help overcome
challenges.

(Re)train your brain

- -

There is nothing worse than to feel stressed about a negative outcome that probably won't happen.

Being haunted by negative thoughts is exhausting and gets you nowhere. It can lower your mood, concentration and energy levels.

If you feel yourself imagining a negative outcome, it's super important to retrain your brain to think how the positive route will turn out.

Make that action a habit.

Take the emotion out

At the start of my business I took situations and feedback very personally.

If things were going wrong, my emotions took over and it was not a good look.

Whether people were being critical or trying to give advice in order to help me improve, I found it hard to be objective.

Eventually it clicked - they were trying to help, or were confused, or upset, or stressed, or reacting because... well, they're human.

So, taking the emotion out is an important skill to learn.

Give yourself the chance to stop, read, think, re read - get a second opinion if needed. But a break to cool off and rationalise and understand that things aren't personal, sometimes it's just business.

You start to see that others who have been in business for a while can seem hard or even ruthless. It doesn't mean they are being unfeeling, just frank and honest in their decision making.

Kill stubborn behaviour

Running your own business means coming up against lots of things you've never done before.

It's also an opportunity to try out new things that you may have been unable to do in your old job.

Public speaking, and presenting in front of my peers was really strange, and I felt the nerves, but after a while it just became part of what I do.

You might be afraid or lack a little confidence but go with it.

Allow yourself to feel weird or awkward for a while - it soon goes.

Adapt and try to be conscious to kill off any stubborn behaviour that holds you back or won't let you try things out.

Adapting your style

Watching others make decisions and deal with circumstances can give you great insights into adapting your own style for better results.

I've learned a lot from this 'people watching', adapting what I learn to make it my own and to see what happens.

Some people just have an amazing way of talking about things, or influencing others. Others have established an awesome business and team culture

Train yourself to watch carefully, and consciously try things out for yourself. If you find they work, keep practicing and it soon becomes second nature.

Personal Finances

Being 'good' with personal finances isn't acceptable when starting a business.

You need to be totally on it.

Your business needs you to be disciplined

You have to be realistic.

Even if you start with nothing, it means your personal spending needs to be on an even tighter budget.

Continuing to adopt this mindset is really important as your business starts to grow.

The minute you make a profit and extra cash, it shouldn't be about how much you can take personally, but more about how much do you need to re-invest to take things to the next level.

I'm not saying don't enjoy yourself, but keep it real and stay balanced.

Your time will come

It can take a while to start making a good living from a new business. Even when you see the money coming in it's important to remember that this belongs to the business not you.

This can be really frustrating, especially as you've worked hard and not seen much reward yet. You just need to be a bit savvy on how, when and how much you take.

Stay grounded, be sensible and take just what you need at first. Remember, just draining the cash could leave you short later with nothing to show for it but a big personal tax bill.

If you're not used to this it can feel quite stressful. The key is to have an adviser or accountant to help you understand the finances of the business and work out how to give you the living you need.

Just keep pushing through. You'll come out of the other side and enjoy the rewards soon enough.

Have a personal goal to aim for

There are lots of things that we want for ourselves or our families.

They may not be physical things either; choosing how you spend your time and having more flexibility is increasingly important to people.

What is important, is you always go back to the big vision, your big motivation, your goal.

Believe in yourself and know you can achieve it.

Whatever your goal is and what reward you take, the focus it will give you can get you through the harder times along the way.

Debt and business

It's essential that both you and the business have the cash needed to keep going even when trading is harder.

You should look to your business to provide first and foremost, and to do that you need to look at cashflow daily as this will help you focus on the sales you need, and where you can limit costs. Once you know where you are, you can take a better view on funding.

Ask yourself some honest questions like how much you need, for how long and how much it will cost?

As the owner you can also think about other actions:

Do you need to get a second job? Can you rent a room out in your house? Or sell any non essential assets?

Regardless you need to know your limits, have contingencies in place (for the unexpected) and a time frame.

Only you can decide on the risk element and how far you are willing to stretch yourself. But, I would try and do everything you can before borrowing.

Squeeze through a cash shortage on your own terms and all the money will be yours and you won't be looking at lengthy repayments.

Eye on the future

Perhaps not top of the list when you are starting out, but you need to think about your future wealth as well as your immediate needs.

When you make enough cash regularly to live and do all the things you love, there is always the question about mortgages, pensions and savings.

It all sounds very heavy, but these are things which will give us the options and flexibility in the future.

Some people like to reinvest into their businesses, others prefer to use extra cash to buy a property. Whatever you choose, they are things which will eventually pay you back - hopefully with a good return!

But you shouldn't sacrifice the very long term at the expense of the present.

So think about your future, yes sure, but also don't forget to enjoy what you have now.

11

Taking Risks

Stepping outside
your comfort zone
has an amazing
impact on how you
view your world.

Risks help you adapt

- -

Pushing yourself to try new things helps to strengthen your mind, even if they seem intimidating to begin with. It also helps you become more resilient

Seriously, what is the worst that can happen?

Taking risks helps you to naturally adapt to circumstances. You learn to see risk as a scary opportunity, not reasons to pull away.

Forgiveness not permission

There are far too many situations in business where it's unnecessarily hard to get *stuff done*.

This can be really frustrating if you're impatient. It's worse when you can see a much better way of doing things but the people around (or above) you aren't budging.

The balance is whether to act now, or make the decision that you will never work in the same way again.

When I was an employee I had to make a call about whether it was better to act and ask for forgiveness or wait and try and get permission.

When you're your own boss, you don't have to ask anyone but you do have to have confidence in your decision.

The question you need to ask is what's at stake if I do this, and what's to lose if I don't?

Be prepared to walk away

Not everything you try works.

There have been many times where something looks perfect, but in the end I just had to walk away.

My early efforts at outsourcing is a great example.

I read a lot about how people used it to help them scale but the reality is that it can be very hit and miss.

It wasn't right and so I pulled the lot, but the concept makes sense and I keep looking at how I can make it work for me.

Being prepared to try also means being prepared to walk away, and the courage to come back at it from a different angle.

Where are YOUR limits

I've pushed what I think are my limits many times.

I always think I can handle it, and it will be fine, but then there are times when I realise "Aaagh, I've agreed to something and now I need to deliver!"

The challenge here is to always make sure you're OK, and not going beyond what you can deal with by yourself.

Your mindset needs to be *reset*, to help you take a step back and ensure that you can deal with what's coming up.

If you can't, get some help.

Bring in consultants where needed and reach out to people who can support you. People you trust, and who can help you either practically or emotionally.

Tick you life goal boxes

Don't hang around waiting to fulfill your life goals.

Make that list and tick off as many as possible.

If I want to head to New Zealand I will, if I want to skydive, I will!

I don't hold back and I hate saying "I can't".

If you say you can't, you won't, if you say you CAN, you more than likely WILL.

Even if it sounds pretty scary, if it's something that you want to do, give it a go!

12

Passion And Resilience

Looking after
your business also
means looking after
your excitement,
your drive, your
happiness, your
health.

Ideas thrill

Exploring new ideas should always be exciting!

It's part of the thrill and satisfaction you get for having a passion for doing what is right for your business

I love innovation, especially in tech, and seeing how this could keep me ahead. So when you find that new service or tool the learning, testing and implementing can be a lot of fun.

But it could just as much be about the development of a new service, or reengineering of an existing one.

Whatever they are, the right ideas can re-energise you as the owner, the company and everyone in it.

What's normal anyway?

- -

Life would be so much easier if you only had growing your business to think about.

But with customers and staff there is always something which comes up - and then there are personal matters like health, finances, family, and friends.

Having all this 'stuff' come at you at once eventually starts to feel normal and juggling it all becomes second nature.

The important thing is how you deal with it.

Find a balance, plan where possible, make decisions on what's important then worry about the rest later.

Health is a priority

One thing that can't wait is your health - your business needs a fit and healthy you to be able to continue, so make sure it is always a priority.

Alone time

-- --

Being around people all the time can be draining, especially when you are the boss and expected to be around for your team.

Sometimes I feel less productive and find myself checking out without realising. So I book time every day to do something different and give myself some space.

I might head to the gym, go out with friends, or book a trip out purely so I can get the chance to get a little distance, and reflect on what's going on.

It's quieter times like this that I can usually see issues, get a handle on errors, and realise what I need to change.

That bit of time alone can be super productive.

Think positive, be happy

Being happy with the decisions you make can take you a long way.

Reflecting on when things haven't gone so well I can see how they impact on my mood, decisions and ability to cope.

However, striving for happiness is important. You can control material things like your home, car, or even place of work.

But with some others you won't be so fortunate.

Just keep focussed and have things in your mind that give you strength.

For me these are: My friends, memories of my mum, my future.

<u>Love</u> what you do

Always have a love for what you do.

When the passion is there it shows in everything and becomes infectious.

Being passionate and leading the way inspires others to be the same; they want to be a part of what you do.

You'll get tested along the way so keep reminding yourself of the reasons why you started in the first place.

Keep falling in love with what you do.

Dedication

Maria Jesus Falcon Huerta
24.11.1948 – 29.03.2007

Seize opportunity, travel the world, be happy and take advantage of the freedom we have today.

This wisdom passed to me from my late mother stays with me always, and especially when I try to find words on how to lead your best life.

The childhood memories and the small things that mattered lead me to become an adult who is free spirited, takes opportunities, sees new places, loves the work that I do and now gets to share the wisdom to help and support others.

Things were not easy for my mother. She struggled with life as a single parent. Supporting us on the bare minimum of cash she said we were very lucky to have an education, to not have to work from a young age, to have a roof over our heads and to have food on our table. Even to have hot water. We couldn't leave food at the table and we learned to appreciate the dinners even if they were the same or very basic.

Even so, we were happy-go-lucky kids. We played outside, we climbed trees, we picnicked together and cycled. Really simple and free things to do as a family with some wonderful memories. Life had no luxuries, yet, when we came home from school she managed to find the pennies to put small gifts on our bed. It was clearly a smart way to get us out of our uniform - but it worked. Living basic lives and being happy worked.

Staying true to yourself and remaining grounded and humble are key things I really see showing in my character as an adult today.

My mum worked really hard, holding down several jobs to take care of us. Over the years she was a seamstress, an interpreter for the courts, a cleaner for some of the wealthy local families, a nursing home carer. She helped out in a mobile cafe and was a dinner lady at our school. And at each, apart from the interpreting, we were somehow involved. We helped out in the cleaning jobs, we went to the nursing homes and we helped stitch a few ties and bags.

When you see the hard work and dedication she put in to making sure we had the basic necessities, it made me work my arse off at school to ensure I got a well paid job so I didn't have the same struggles and make her proud.

One thing I know, she was a strong independent woman, who strived to make sure she did all she could for her children and I will be forever grateful.

When I wrote this book, every part of it had her in mind.

About

Alex Falcon Huerta FCCA

As an accountant working with some of the most agile and progressive small businesses in the UK, Alex has built Soaring Falcon Accountancy into an award winning business serving clients in the UK and internationally.

Her reputation for being at the forefront of tech adoption and having a unique energetic style, has seen her become an eye-catching member of the accounting profession, and gained her the opportunity to represent both the ACCA and small business to HM Government.

Although dedicated to serving her local community in Bedford, her clients come from a range of sectors and particularly high growth technology companies.

List of awards and achievements since launching Soaring Falcon in 2015

Women & Broadband Business Awards - 'Most Outstanding Achievement' - 2016

2020 Innovation - 'Best New Cloud Practice' - 2016

Xero's 'Most Valued Professional' - 2017

British Accountancy Awards - 'New practice of the year'- 2018

Practice Ignitions 'Top 50 Women In Accounting' - 2018

ACCA 'UK outstanding contribution' - 2018

British Accounting Marketing Awards - "Rising Star" - 2018

Other things to add to the mix:-

ACCA Advocate - MoU with Xero

ACCA - International Assembly Member Since 2018

ACCA global technology forum member

All-Party Parliamentary Group - International trade and technology - 2018

UK Pacesetter - Xero and ACCA

Keynote Speaker for the Finance and Accounting Industry

Accounting Web Columnist

Shortlisted for :

Innovative firm of the year Accounting Excellence 2018

Innovative and digital firm of the year Accounting Excellence 2020

SME Luton & Bedfordshire Business Awards - Bedford Business of the Year 2020

SME Luton & Bedfordshire Business Awards - Bedford Innovative firm of the year 2020

Women in Accounting and Finance Awards: Role Model of the year 2020

- -

Websites

www.alexfalconhuerta.com
www.soaring-falcon.com
Twitter: @alexmfalcon
Insta: alexfalconhuertafcca

...and with thanks to Richard Sergeant, Principle Point.

X - X - MMXX

Lightning Source UK Ltd.
Milton Keynes UK
UKHW050741160822
407365UK00001B/1